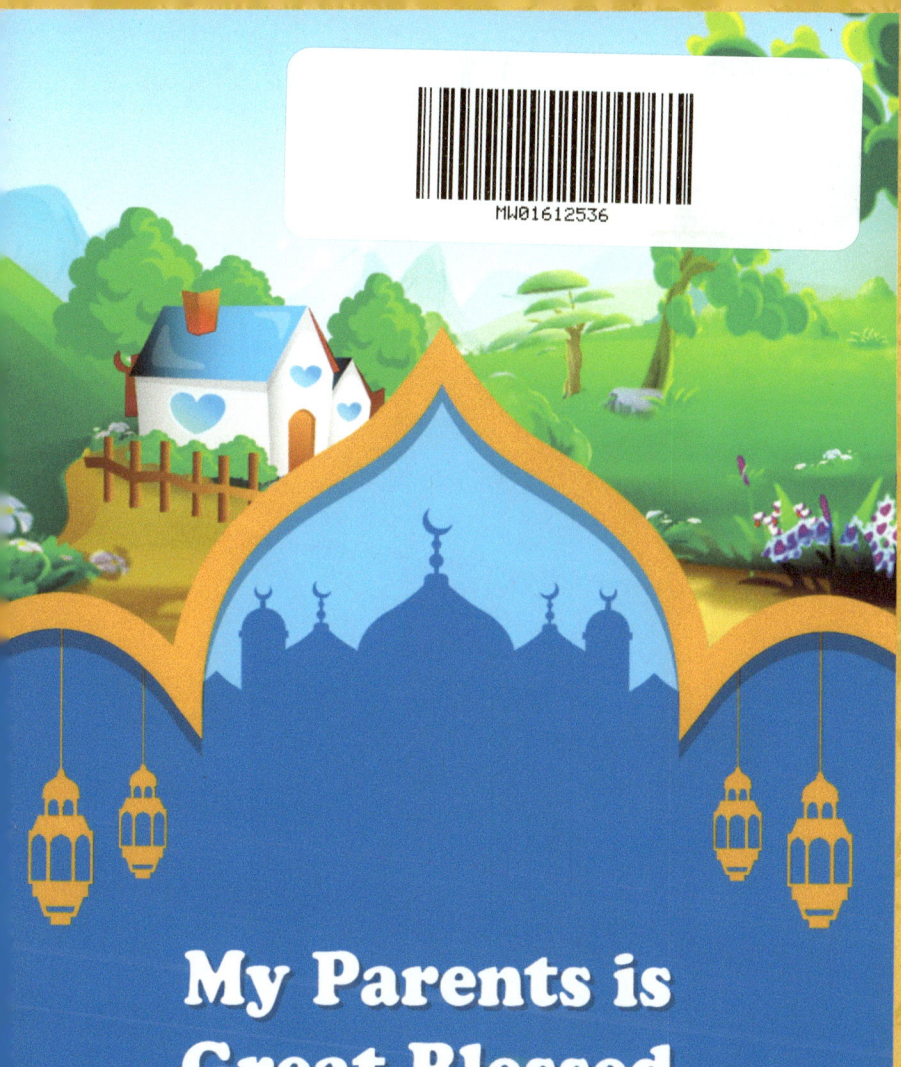

My Parents is
Great Blessed
from Allah Ta'ala

Islamic Book for Kids
Series One

Our Parents is a great blessed gave us from Allah Ta'ala They take care of us

When we were baby they awake
whole night for us and
take care for us
When we cried they came to us
as soon as they heard

They fed us every time
when we hungry
They have made us strong now see how
strong and big we are today
They helped us to crawl and walk
and teach us how to talk

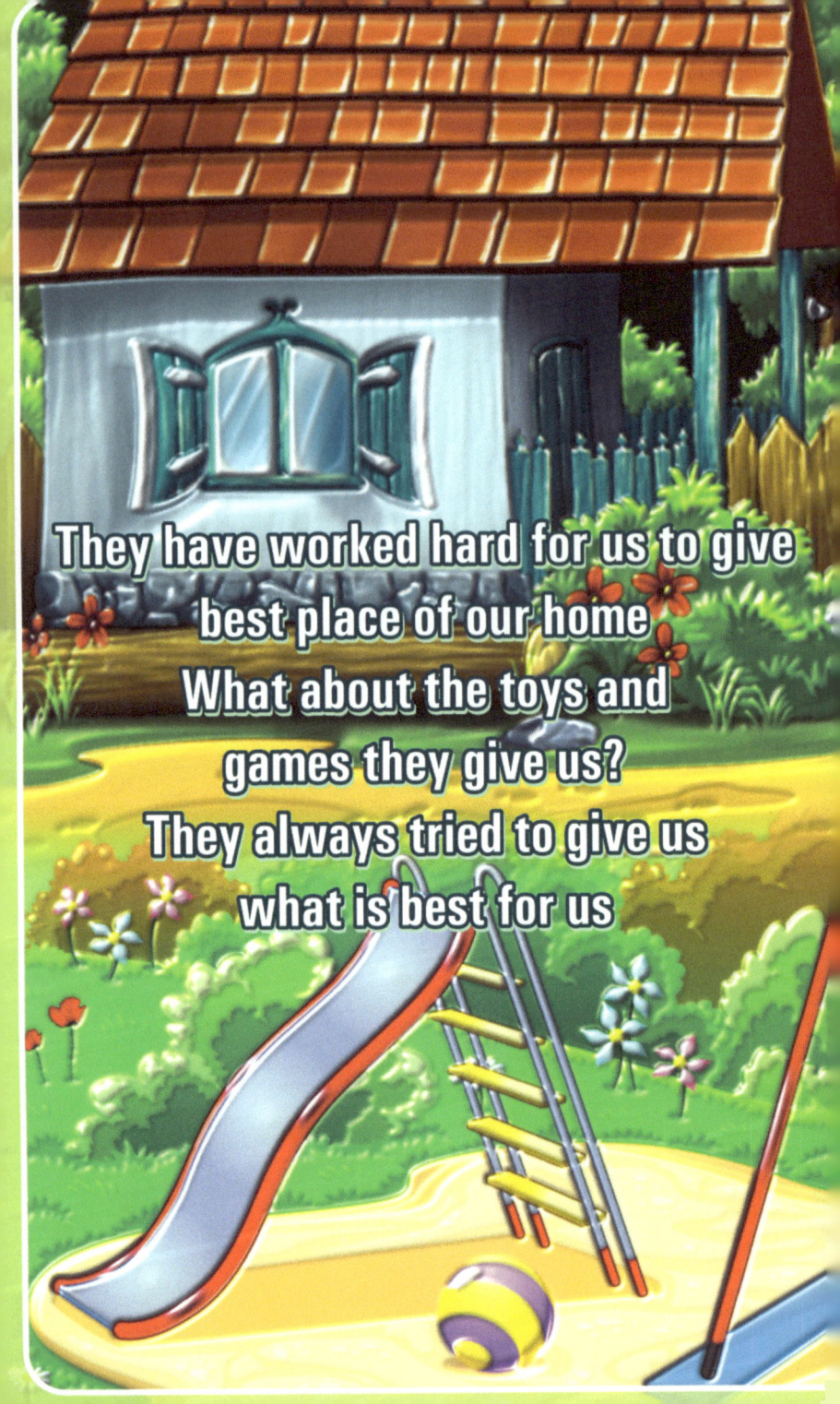

They have worked hard for us to give
best place of our home
What about the toys and
games they give us?
They always tried to give us
what is best for us

They give us bath every day and
feed when we ask for food
They wash our clothes every day and
make sure we always clean and smell nice

When we are sick they look after us
and take care and more concern
about us themselves
They make dua to Allah Ta'ala
that makes us
better because they know it is only
Allāh Ta'ala who can
give us cure

They make dua to Allah Ta'ala that makes us good children and obedient to Allah Ta'ala every time That is why they always recite following verses of Noble Quran, "My Lord! Grant me (children) from the righteous"

They taught us how to read and write
so we can able to learn Islam, know
Allah Ta'ala and know how to
live our lives by Islamic way

They taught us about Allah Ta'ala,
Angel, heaven and hell
They taught us book of Allah Ta'ala and
messengers who brought them
They taught us about
Prophets Muhammad [PBUH] and
his family and the companions
They taught us to read, write and
recite the Noble Quran

Our parents told us how our prophets
Muhammad [PBUH]
taught us about to being good Muslims and
how we did good deed to please
Allah Ta'ala so we will go to Jannah

Our parents told us how our prophets Muhammad [PBUH] warned about the bad actions that will displease Allah Ta'ala.
In this knowledge how we can protect ourselves from the punishment of the hellfire

They want us to learn good manners so that we will behave well to each other and being good Muslim children.
We need to always thankful and grateful to our parents

Allah Ta'ala has place love and mercy into
our parents heart for us in the return of this mercy and
kindness we need to love and kind to be our parents

Allah Ta'ala says in the Noble Quran,

"And we have enjoined on man to be dutiful and
kind to his parents..." [Surah Luqman v.14]

Allah Ta'ala has promised to us great rewards for being good to parents.

The Messenger [PBUH] of AllahTa'ala said,

"The parents are the middle door among the doors of paradise,

you can lose it or win it if you wish"

We need to always respect to our parents
We need to try not to make them sad and angry,
no to being rude to them or disobedient
If we did something wrong or upset them then
we must tell them we are sorry and promise them
not to do bad thing again

When our parents get old then we must need to take care of them with the patience & love
We should thank them for look after when we child and need to make dua to Allah Ta'ala for them
Allah Ta'ala asked us to make dua for our parents by saying

CPSIA information can be obtained
at www.ICGtesting.com
Printed in the USA
LVHW070326290121
677806LV00001B/4

* 9 7 8 4 8 2 1 0 9 7 5 7 9 *